W9-BDQ-203

Rookie
Read-About Science®

Where Land Meets Sea

By Allan Fowler

Consultants

Linda Cornwell, Learning Resource Consultant,
Indiana Department of Education

Fay Robinson, Child Development Specialist

Lynne Kepler, Educational Consultant

Children's Press®
A Division of Grolier Publishing
New York   London   Hong Kong   Sydney
Danbury, Connecticut

Project Editor: Downing Publishing Services
Designer: Herman Adler Design Group
Photo Researcher: Caroline Anderson

Library of Congress Cataloging-in-Publication Data

Fowler, Allan.
    Where land meets sea / by Allan Fowler.
       p. cm. – (Rookie read-about science)
    Includes index.
    Summary: Examines different kinds of seashores, sandy, marshy, and
rocky, and discusses how they can change over time.
      ISBN 0-516-20322-3 (lib.bdg.)   ·   0-516-26155-X (pbk.)
      1. Seashore—Juvenile literature. [l. Seashore.] I. Title. II. Series
GB453.F68   1997   98-26984
551.4'57–dc20   CIP
                                                      AC

Many families spend summer vacations by the seashore.

They head for wide,
sandy beaches that are
great for swimming . . .
or surfing . . .

or boating . . . or just lying
in the sun. But there are
other kinds of seashores
besides sandy beaches.

A seashore is any place
where land meets sea
or ocean. Some seashores
are rocky. They may look
lonely, yet be full of life.

Animals and plants live
in little pools, called tide
pools, among the rocks.

Steep cliffs can be found
behind many rocky shores.

Or a cliff might rise
directly out of the water.

Some seashores are
marshes, thick with tall
reeds and other plants
growing in the salty
sea water.

Great numbers of fish
live in these salt marshes.

Certain trees, such as
mangroves, can grow
in salt water.

There are muddy seashores, too. People dig for clams in mud flats or sandy beaches.

Not all beaches have fine sand . . . the sand that feels so nice and soft under your feet when you run on it.

There are pebbly and
stony beaches. You
wouldn't want to run
barefoot on one of those.

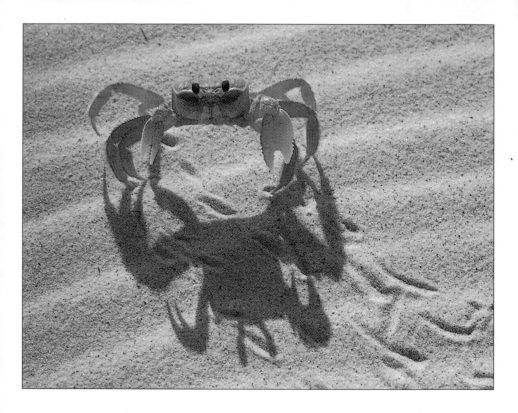

Crabs are at home on
beaches as well as in the
water. Some kinds of crabs
run sideways.

Gulls, pelicans, and many other birds fly and nest along shores.

gull   oystercatcher

Pelicans have big pouches under their beaks, where they store the fish they have caught.

Seashores are always changing their shape. Waves rolling in from the sea wear away cliffs, and make caves in the rock. That takes a very long time.

Sandy beaches change much more quickly.

Just one heavy storm can wash away most of a beach.

Waves and winds shift sand from place to place.

Sand may pile up to form a long offshore island, called a sand bar. The bar then protects the shoreline from the waves.

Breakwaters are walls that people build in the water. They slow down the waves and help keep the sand from being carried out to sea.

A big river can change
a shoreline. The river
carries silt — bits of
rock and soil —

which forms new land
where the river meets
the sea. This new land
is called a delta.

There are many ways to enjoy yourself at a seashore, whether it's sandy or rocky, muddy or marshy.

Besides swimming or sailing,
you can go fishing . . .
collect seashells . . . or see
how many different forms
of animal life you can find.

And many people feel
good just breathing
that sea air, with its
salty tang . . .

and listening to the roar
of the waves.

Words You Know

beach

cliff

delta

seashore

pelicans

marsh   reeds

mangrove

crab

sand bar

breakwater

31

Index

About the Author

Allan Fowler is a free-lance writer with a background in advertising.
Born in New York, he lives in Chicago now and enjoys traveling.

Photo Credits

Dembinsky Photo Associates — ©Darrell Gulin, cover; ©Bill Lea, 11, 31 (top right); ©Carl R. Sams, II, 17 (background); ©Sharon Cummings, 26

Photo Researchers, Inc. — ©Bachmann, 3; ©Spencer Grant, 6, 30 (bottom right); ©George Ranalli, 8; ©Michael P. Gadomski, 15; ©Dan Guravich, 16, 31 (middle right); ©Jack Dermid, 17 (inset); ©Richard R. Hansen, 18, 31 (top left); ©Charles E. Mohr, 19; ©David Weintraub, 21; ©F. Gohier, 22, 31 (bottom left); ©Calvin Larsen, 24-25, 30 (bottom left)

Tony Stone Images, Inc. — ©Frank Orel, 4-5, 30 (top left); ©Sylvain Grandadam, 23, 31 (bottom right); ©Claudia Kunin, 29

Norbert Wu — ©Brandon Cole/Mo Yung Productions, 7, 27; ©Norbert Wu, 9, 30 (top right)

Gerry Ellis Nature Photography, 12, 31 (middle left)

Peter Arnold, Inc. — ©Chlaus Lotscher, 13

©SuperStock International, Inc. — 14

COVER: Cape Kiwanda on the Oregon coast

DUE DATE			